PART ONE

Laura and Grandpa

Discovering Science Together

by Dr. Robert H. Krupp

the Peppertree Press

Sarasota, Florida

For information regarding permission, call 941-922-2662
or contact us at our website: www.peppertreepublishing.com
or write to: the Peppertree Press, LLC.
Attention: Publisher
1269 First Street, Suite 7
Sarasota, Florida 34236

ISBN: 978-1-936343-96-6
Library of Congress Number: 2011931059
Printed in the U.S.A.
Printed June 2011

DEDICATION

This series of **Laura and Grandpa** books are dedicated to
Edward Stratemeyer (October 4, 1862—May 10, 1930).

In 1910 he began the **Tom Swift** series, which totaled over 100
volumes. In the 1930s and early '40s, I read many of these books.
They made me aware of how science, technology, and invention
can be of benefit to society. These books bred and instilled in me
a life-long spirit of learning, a zest to discover the unknown, and a
passion for adventure.

I hope that the **Laura and Grandpa** books will so too inspire the
young and old who read them.

ACKNOWLEDGMENTS

A special word of appreciation to Dr. Janice Bolt, who gave me the inspiration to write a children's book on science.

My undying gratitude goes to Shirley Silverman, Flo de Jesu Donatelli, Nancy Boltwood, and Ellen Orr, who provided many valuable suggestions while editing the initial manuscripts.

I am truly grateful and blest to have such wonderful friends as Claudia Deschu, Kim "Charisma" Hoffman, Guy Cannata, Cliff Boltwood, Bill Aleman, Brady Hendricks, Joe Schmidt, and Brenda & Bill Fasciano, all great people, who encouraged me every step of the way to pursue this dream and make it a reality.

Very, very special words of appreciation are extended to Dr. Awatif Soliman, my scientific advisor and mentor. She was invaluable in many aspects along the way.

And how can I ever thank my daughters, Colleen and Christine, and grandchildren, Laura and Austin, for their inspiration and encouragement to "get it done."

Finally, I wish to acknowledge my indebtedness and gratitude to the thousands of students with whom I have interacted over the past six decades. They, more than anyone else, have helped to "teach the teacher" and prepare me to take on this task. Thank you, all!

Table of Contents

The Egg

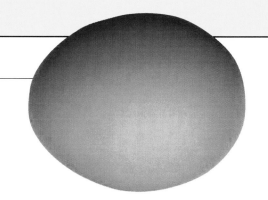

One day Laura, Mom, and Dad drove to Grandma and Grandpa's house for an overnight visit. When they got out of the car, Laura ran over to her Nana and Papa to give them a big hug and kiss.

The next morning Laura sat at the table in the kitchen. While she drank her milk, Nana cooked some scrambled eggs for breakfast. Papa came to the table with his coffee and newspaper. "Good morning, Laura! How did you sleep last night?" he asked.

"Morning, Papa! I slept just fine," she replied.

"What's Grandma cooking for you, Laura?" Papa asked.

"Scrambled eggs", she said. "I love scrambled eggs."

"Where did Nana get the eggs?" he asked.

"Don't be silly, Papa, she got them from the fridge."

"You're right, but where did she get them to put into the fridge?"

"From the store," answered Laura.

"Now you've got it. However, I wonder—where did the store get the eggs?"

Laura thought for a bit, and then her eyes lit up. She smiled and said, "From the farmer!"

"Of course, but do you know where the farmer got them?" asked Papa.

"From a chicken," she said.

"Very good," Papa said smiling.

Papa then went to the fridge and came back with a raw egg. "Can you tell me if this egg is fresh?" he asked Laura.

"I'm not sure Papa. I think it's fresh because you just got it out of the fridge," Laura answered.

"Well, let's test it to see if it is fresh," suggested Papa.

Papa asked Laura to get a large bowl and fill it about half full with cold water. "Then bring it there," he said.

Laura brought the bowl of cold water to the table.

"What now Papa?" she asked.

"Carefully place this egg into the bowl and tell me what you see?" said Papa.

"The egg is lying on its side at the bottom of the bowl," Laura said.

"That's good," said Papa, "because now we know that this egg is fresh. If the egg had floated with its pointy end down that would mean the egg is old, but we could still use it for scrambled eggs. However, if it had totally floated we'd throw it out because it would be rotten!"

Grandma brought a plate of scrambled eggs and toast to the table. "Here you are Laura," she said.

"Thanks, Nana. Could I have some more milk, please?"

"Of course dear," Nana said as she poured milk into Laura's glass.

While she was eating her breakfast, Papa said, "Laura, have you ever seen colored eggs?"

"Yes," she said, "at Easter time."

"Did you ever color any eggs?" Papa asked.

"Yes, I helped Mommy twice. That was a lot of fun!" recalled Laura.

"Did your Mommy cook the eggs before you colored them?"

"Yes, she cooked them in boiling water to make them hard."

"Good. Did you ever eat one of these colored eggs?"

"Yes, but first I had to get the egg out of the shell."

"When you removed the shell, what did the egg look like?"

"It was white and had a yellow center."

"Do you know the name of the yellow center?"

"I think it's called a **yolk**. Is that right?"

"Absolutely! The other part of the egg is often called the white of the egg. The name for it is **albumin**."

Papa took the raw egg out of the bowl of water. As he dried it with a paper towel, he said, "Laura, do you think you could take the egg out of its shell without breaking the shell or putting a hole in it?"

"I don't think so."

"Well, let's try."

He went to a cabinet and got out a clear glass jar. After carefully putting the raw egg in the jar, he poured white vinegar over the egg until it was covered.

"Let's leave this alone for awhile," said Papa.

While they waited, Laura went to her coloring book to make a picture of a colored egg for Grandma. Papa went into the family room to finish reading his paper.

Later that afternoon while having lunch, he said, "Laura, what's happening to our egg in the jar?"

Going over to the counter Laura looked at the egg. "There are some tiny bubbles on the shell," Laura said.

"Good! Carefully touch the jar to see if it is hot like a pot of boiling water."

"No, it isn't hot!" Laura said after touching the jar.

"That's fine! The bubbles you see didn't come from boiling the vinegar. Let's leave this egg alone for now. We will look at it tomorrow," Papa said.

The next morning after breakfast, Papa told Laura to look at their special egg. "Tell me what you see today, Laura."

"It looks like the shell is gone. I see something jellylike with the yellow yolk in the middle. Is the egg cooked? What happened to it, Papa?" asked Laura.

"No, the egg is not cooked. It is still a raw egg, but the shell is gone. Here's what happened . . ."

"Vinegar is a weak **acid**. Oranges, lemons, and limes are also weak **acids**. I am sure you have eaten these things. How do these fruits taste to you, Laura?"

Laura made a face and said, "I like oranges, but the lemons and limes taste sour to me."

Papa continued, "The sourness you taste is a result of the juices being **acids**. An acid is a chemical that is dissolved in water, which gives it a sour taste. There are many different kinds of acids. Some of them are weak and some of them are strong. Vinegar and all those fruit juices are weak **acids**. We can eat them and they do not hurt us," he explained.

Papa went on. "But the strong **acids**—you never, ever should taste or drink them! You must be very careful when you handle them because they will burn your skin. These strong acids are found in cleaning products your Mommy or Daddy might use."

"Now let's get back to our egg," Papa said. "The shell is made of things called **calcium**, **carbon**, and **oxygen**. Have you heard of any of these, Laura?"

"I think so," replied Laura. "My doctor told me that my bones are made of **calcium**. Mommy tells me to drink a lot of milk, which has **calcium**, so it will help to strengthen my bones."

"Good. Anything else?" asked Papa.

Laura thought, "I'm not sure if I remember it right. I think my teacher told me that the black part of my pencil is **carbon**. She also said that every time I take a breath of air, I take **oxygen** into my lungs."

"Excellent! You have a very good teacher! Now let's finish talking about what happened to the egg."

"Vinegar, the weak acid, changes the egg shell. The acid eats away at the shell until it disappears. During this time a gas made of **carbon** and **oxygen** forms. You saw bubbles of this gas on the shell yesterday. Examples of other gasses are air and **helium**, a gas which fills up a balloon and makes it float," Papa explained.

"The jelly-like material you now see is not changed by the vinegar. That is why it and the yolk remain. So you did what you thought couldn't be done. The egg is out of the shell, but we didn't break the shell or put a hole in it. How about that?" said Papa.

"That's just great, Papa! What are we going to do next week when I visit?"

"Ummm . . . Well Laura let me give it some thought."

Curds and Whey

O
n a beautiful summer day, Laura and Grandpa sat on the front porch swing sipping a glass of milk.

Papa asked Laura, "Do you know the story of Little Miss Muffet?"

Laura smiled and said,

> *"Little Miss Muffet sat on a tuffet,*
> *eating her curds and whey.*
> *Along came a spider,*
> *who sat down beside her*
> *and frightened Miss Muffet away."*

"So, what's a **tuffet**? What are **curds** and **whey**?" Papa asked.

"I don't know, Papa. What are they?"

"A **tuffet** is an old English word for a 3-legged stool, Laura. Let's go inside and see if we can figure out what **curds** and **whey** are."

They went into the kitchen. While Laura sat down, Papa brought to the table some skim milk, two plastic glasses, a coffee filter, white vinegar, a funnel, baking soda, a measuring cup, and an eyedropper.

"What now, Papa?" asked Laura.

Papa replied, "Pour ½ cup of the milk into the measuring cup. When we do this, we must be sure to use skim milk. Then pour it into one of the glasses."

"OK. I've done that. What's next?"

"Go to the sink and rinse the measuring cup in water. Come back here and measure out ⅛ cup of vinegar. Add it to the milk in the glass. Stir the vinegar and milk with a spoon. After that, we'll leave it alone for a few minutes."

Laura drank some more milk while Papa had a cup of coffee. Then they both looked at the glass with the milk and vinegar. "What do you see now?" Papa asked.

"I see some clumps of white stuff floating in the milk."

"Very good! The clumps of white material are curds. Let's go away for awhile longer."

After an hour Papa and Laura went to look at the glass with the mixture of milk and vinegar. "Laura, I want you to put the coffee filter into the funnel. Then place the funnel on top of the clean glass. Carefully pour the milk and curds into the coffee filter."

"Do you see the cloudy liquid that drained down into the second glass, Laura?"

"Yes," said Laura. "I see it."

"That liquid in the glass below the funnel is called whey. Lift the funnel off of the glass. Hold onto the coffee filter with your fingers. Turn the funnel upside down over the first glass and dump the curds back into the first glass. Use the spoon to scrape the curds into the glass."

"Add ½ teaspoon of baking soda to the curds and stir it a bit. It is dry, so let's add a few drops of water from the eye dropper. But first, you will need to draw some water from this cup of water into the eye dropper."

"Gently touch the **curds** and see how they feel."

"They are very sticky, Papa."

8

"Yes, they are! You just made some glue from the curds. Let's test and see how good your glue is. Take these strips of paper and see if your glue will hold them together."

Laura did what her Papa told her. She then said, "It worked! The paper is stuck together!"

"Great! Now how would you like a Miss Muffet's Curds and Whey Salad for lunch?"

"Well, I'm not sure if I would like it. Does it smell and taste like **vinegar**? I'll try a little bit if you make it."

Laura watched as Papa washed some lettuce leaves. He dried them with a paper towel and placed them on two plates. "The leaves of lettuce will be our tuffets," he said."

Papa took a container of cottage cheese out of the fridge. He put a ½ cup of cottage cheese on each plate and said, "I didn't tell you this before, but the way farmers make cottage cheese is very much like what we have done today. So the cottage cheese will be our curds."

"Laura, would you like a large or small spider on your curds?"

"Yuk! I don't like spiders. But if you put one on, make it a tiny one. And put it on the side, please."

"That's fine. Here's a raisin on the side of your salad for a tiny spider.

I don't mind a big spider, so here's a prune on top of mine."

As Papa placed the salad in front of Laura he said, "Bon appétit! Do you know what that means?"

"I think that's French for 'Enjoy your meal.' How do you say thank you in French, Papa?"

"Merci Beaucoup!" he replied.

"Merci Beaucoup! Thank you for this nice salad, Papa."

"You're welcome!"

As she ate her salad, Laura said "I can't wait until next week to see what exciting project you have for us to do together, Papa."

REFERENCE - Miss Muffet's Curds and Whey Salad is from *Mother Goose Cookbook*, © 1998, Gloria T. Delamar.

The Cabbage

O ne morning, Laura was sitting at the kitchen table drawing on some paper with her crayons. Her cousin Austin was also at the table drinking a glass of milk.

Grandpa came into the kitchen carrying a small bag.

"Hi Papa! How are you?" Laura asked.

"I'm feeling just great! How are you two doing?"

"We're fine," Austin said. "I am staying here for a few days while my mom and dad are on a trip."

"I knew that," said Papa.

"What have you got in the bag?" Laura asked. "Some treats?"

"Here Austin, take it out. What is it?"

"It's a cabbage," he said, saddened that it wasn't cookies or candy.

"Right, but what color is it?"

"It's a red cabbage," said Laura.

While they were talking, Papa went to the cabinet and brought a pot, chopping board, and a small vegetable cleaver to the table.

"What are we going to do?" Austin asked.

"We're going to boil some cabbage. I'm glad you are here today, Austin. You can help us." Papa then cut the cabbage in half and put one portion aside.

10

"Laura and I will rip off some leaves from this ½ of the cabbage. Austin, you carefully slice the leaves into thin strips."

After shredding and cutting up the cabbage, they placed all the pieces into the pot.

Papa asked Austin to take the pot to the sink. "Cover the cabbage with cold water and bring it to the stove, please," said Papa.

As he lit the burner, Papa said, "We'll boil the water for about 25-30 minutes. The liquid in the pot should turn blue or dark purple. Then we'll turn off the burner and let everything cool down."

Later that morning when the pot, water, and cabbage were cool enough to handle, they all came back to the kitchen.

Papa brought the pot with the cabbage, a strainer, and large jar to the table.

"Austin, hold this strainer over the jar while I pour the juice and cabbage into the strainer. While we're doing this, Laura, I want you to find a plastic container so we can store something in the fridge."

After collecting the juice in the jar, Papa put the cabbage from the strainer into the plastic container Laura had brought him.

Papa sealed the container with a lid. "Laura, put this in the fridge and later, I will add a little vinegar to it. Then we can put this cabbage on a hot dog or a salad."

Papa brought 10 cups, 2 eye droppers, and a pitcher of water to the table.

"Laura, fill two cups with water until they are nearly full. Leave two of the cups empty. Finally, fill the remaining cups halfway with water," Papa instructed.

"While she's doing that, Austin, get a can of clear soda or carbonated water out of the fridge. Pour the soda into

one of the empty cups until it is half-full." Austin did as Papa asked.

"Now Laura, in the cups half-filled with water, I want you to add a few drops of five different things. In the first cup, add four or five drops of white vinegar. After that, rinse your eye dropper, inside and out. You can use the water in one of the full cups for your rinse water."

"To the second cup, add four or five drops of lemon juice making sure to clean the eyedropper in the cup of rinse water when you are finished."

"In the third cup, add four or five drops of soap detergent and in the fourth cup, add four to five drops of liquid hand soap. Finally, in the fifth cup add four or five drops of hair shampoo, rinsing the eye dropper between using a new liquid."

"While she is doing that Austin, put a ½ teaspoon of baking soda into one of the cups that is half full of water. Don't put anything in the cup with the soda. Be careful to leave one full cup of water with nothing else in it. We don't want this water used for rinsing out the eyedropper."

As Laura and Austin were adding different things to the cups of water, Papa went to a drawer and brought a handful of small spoons to the table. "With a small spoon, gently stir each cup into which you put something. Be sure to use a different spoon for each cup. You do not have the stir the water in the cup of pure water."

As Laura and Austin stirred the different cups, Papa carefully poured cabbage juice into the empty cup.

He said, "Now once again, wash out your eyedroppers in our rinse water. Draw up some cabbage juice from the cup. Put about four or five drops of the juice into each cup containing the vinegar, lemon juice, soda, and so on. Be sure you put some drops of the juice into the cup of clear, pure water. You do not have to put any cabbage juice into the cup of rinse water."

"Tell me what you see," Papa said.

"The juice changed color," cried out Laura and Austin.

"Let me know what color each one turned to and I will write it down. Then we can look at a record of what we have seen."

As Laura and Austin told him the different colors, Papa wrote:

"All right, Papa, what's going on?" Laura and Austin asked.

"The cabbage juice we made is what we call an **indicator.** If something is an acid, the cabbage juice will turn pink. A base is the opposite of an acid. If something is a base, the cabbage juice turns green. Water is not an **acid** or a **base**, it is **neutral**, and so it didn't change the color."

"Would you like to do some other fun things with our cabbage juice?"

"Yes. What can we do?"

Papa took some coffee filters and soaked them into the cabbage juice. He laid them flat on a kitchen counter. "We need to let these filters dry out. Laura, will you and Austin watch over these filters for a few days? Don't let anyone throw them out."

"Sure." she said. "I can do that."

"I will put a lid on this jar of cabbage juice and put it into the fridge. It should last about one to two weeks if you keep it cold."

"Now would you two like a little lunch? How about a hot dog? I'm going to put a little vinegar on the boiled cabbage we made today. Along with some mustard and catsup, I'll add this cabbage to my hot dog. Would you like to try that?"

"Sounds good to me," said Austin. "I'm hungry!"

"Me too," chirped Laura. "And maybe we can have some ice cream for dessert."

"I think we can do that," laughed Papa.

	SUBSTANCE	**COLOR**
1.	Clear soda	Pink
2.	Vinegar	Pink
3.	Lemon juice	Pink
4.	Soap detergent	Green
5.	Hand soap	Green
6.	Hair shampoo	Green
7.	Baking soda	Green
8.	Pure water	No color change

Cabbage Paper

Two days after making the juice from a red cabbage, Papa walked into Laura's kitchen. He was carrying a large bag from the market, which he placed into the fridge.

Laura and Austin were outside playing in the yard with Sherlock, Laura's dog. Papa called to them, "Hi, Laura and Austin! Come on in. How's our cabbage paper doing?"

"The filter papers are all dried out. They're in my room," said Laura. "I'll go get them."

While Laura went to get the cabbage paper, Papa asked Austin to help him carry some things to the kitchen table.

They brought some cups, cotton swabs, vinegar, liquid detergent and water to the table.

Laura came in with the dried coffee filters and sat down at the table.

Papa said, "Laura, put vinegar into one of the cups. Austin, pour a half cup of water into another cup and add some detergent and stir it up a bit."

After they did this, Papa said, "Each of you take one of the cabbage papers and spread it out flat on the table in front of you."

"Take a cotton swab. Dip it into the vinegar. Use the swab like a pencil and write your first name on the cabbage paper. After that, use a different swab and dip it into the cup with the liquid detergent. With that one, write your last name on the cabbage paper."

"Wow", said Austin. "This is neat! I see my name in pink and green."

"Good! Now try this," said Papa. "Use the swab with the detergent to carefully trace over your first name. You may need to dip the swab into the detergent cup to get more fluid. After

that, use the first swab with the vinegar to trace over your last name. Tell me what you see."

"This is fun", said Laura. "My name faded and disappeared."

"Excellent," remarked Papa. "Here's is something else you can do. Get another sheet of the cabbage paper and use the swabs and draw some images onto your paper."

While Laura and Austin were drawing images on the cabbage paper Papa went to the fridge. He took out the bag he had placed there earlier. Out of the bag he took an apple, an orange, a lemon, a lime, a pineapple, a peach, a nectarine, a mango, and two strawberries.

"OK. I want you to stop drawing for awhile. I brought all this fruit here so that we can have a nice fruit salad. As I cut up all these fruits, I will give you a piece of each to taste. But before you eat it, rub a strip of our special cabbage paper over each slice I give you. Tell me what you see."

"Gosh—some of the strips of paper changed to pink", said Laura. "Why is that Papa?"

"Do you remember the story I told you about The Egg, Laura? At that time you found out about weak acids and strong acids. The juice of many of the fruit slices I gave you are acids. That is what changed the color of your cabbage paper."

"I didn't know working with cabbage juice could be such fun," smiled Austin.

"Well, it's how you look at it. Some people don't know you can have fun with cabbage juice. The other day I put a jar of cabbage juice into the fridge and if you want, you can always make more cabbage paper from this juice."

"This was just great, Papa! What are we going to do next week?" asked Laura.

"Right now I don't know so I'll have to think about that. Would you like a little snack? How about a nice fruit salad?"

"That sounds good to me," said Austin.

Laura went back to drawing on her cabbage paper. In the meantime, Austin helped Papa make a delicious fruit salad.

Colored Pens

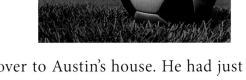

One Saturday afternoon, Papa and Laura drove over to Austin's house. He had just come home from playing soccer that morning.

"Hi Austin! How did your soccer match go?" Papa asked.

"Aw, we lost again," grumbled Austin. "I had two shots at the goal. One hit the crossbar and almost went in. But their goalie caught it," said Austin. "Hi, Laura!" he waved.

"Hi, Austin! Sorry you didn't win—maybe next time," said Laura.

As they all walked into the kitchen, Austin noticed that Papa was carrying a small bag.

"What have you got in the bag?" Austin asked.

"Sorry, no treats. Just some fun things to do this afternoon."

"Austin, we'll wait in the kitchen while you wash up and change your clothes. When you come back, bring some paper clips."

While Austin was gone, Papa and Laura prepared things at the kitchen table. Out of the bag he took four felt tipped pens. Two were green, the other two were black.

Then he took out some cone-shaped coffee filters.

"Laura, please bring some saucers and a pitcher of water to the table," Papa asked.

Austin came back into the kitchen. After getting a bottle of water to drink, he sat down at the table.

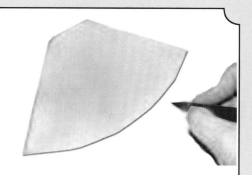

Papa handed a green and black pen to Laura. The other two pens he gave to Austin.

Then Papa said, "These felt tipped pens are water-soluble. I want each of you take a coffee filter. Fold it flat on the table, with the longer rounded end towards you."

"These coffee filters are made for Melitta coffeemakers. They will work best for what we are going to do today. I have found that some filters are either too thin or too wrinkled, so we must use a type like these," Papa said.

"Now use your green pen to make a thick, dark line about one inch long. It should be about ½ inch above the rounded edge of the filter paper. The line should curve along the rounded edge," said Papa.

"Next, use your black pen to make another thick, dark line about one inch long. This line should be next to your green line. The two lines should be far enough apart so that they do not touch each other."

"After the ink dries, pick up the filter paper. Twist it so that it looks like an upside-down ice cream cone. Use a paper clip to hold the edges together. This will help to keep its cone shape."

"Each of you get a saucer and fill it with a little water. Place your filter cone in the saucer with the pointy end upwards. The water in the saucer should be below your pen lines," explained Papa.

"We need to leave this alone for awhile. Let's take a walk. Maybe we can find a place to get an ice cream cone."

About an hour later, Papa, Laura, and Austin returned to the kitchen. Each of them was finishing an ice cream cone.

"Look at the coffee filter sitting in the water. Tell me what you see," said Papa.

"I see purple, orange, yellow, and pink tracks of colors. They seem to come from the black ink," said Laura.

"I see blue and yellow trails, which look like they came from the green line," said Austin.

"What happened?" Laura and Austin asked together.

"As I told you earlier, these pens are water-soluble markers," said Papa. "The black ink is made up of several colors, such as dark blue, yellow, orange, and pink. The green ink is mostly made up of blue and yellow colors."

"The filter paper soaks up water from the saucer. When the water reaches the ink, it starts to dissolve these colors. The colors separate and move to different heights up the coffee filter," explained Papa.

"The chemicals that make up the colors are different from each other. Some of them are lighter than others. Usually, the lighter-weighing chemicals move faster. It is these lighter chemicals that go higher up on the coffee filter," Papa said.

"The colors are very pretty," said Laura.

"Here are more coffee filters," said Papa. "You could try drawing some figures higher up on the cone. Then see what happens as the water rises up to your drawing."

"This is almost like drawing with water colored paints," said Austin.

"I'm going out on the front porch to read my book," said Papa. "You can continue to work with these pens and the coffee filters. Have fun!"

The Candle

It was dark and rainy when Laura came home from school.

In the kitchen, she saw Grandpa having a cup of tea. "Hi, Papa," she said.

"Hi, Laura. How was school today?" smiled Papa.

"School was just fine. I'm all wet. I'm going to change my clothes," said Laura.

When she came back, there were some cookies and a glass of milk on the kitchen table. Papa had put them there for her.

As she sat down he said, "Wait a minute before you start on your cookies. I just want to make it a little nicer in here."

He put a candleholder, some candles, a wide-mouth jar, and a saucer onto the table.

"Laura, whatever I show you now, I don't want you to try this by yourself. Have your Mommy or Daddy help you, if you want to do this again. Do you understand?" asked Papa.

"OK, Papa," said Laura, "go ahead and show me what you want to do."

After lighting one of the candles, he placed it into a candleholder at the center of the table. "There, isn't that nice to have your cookies by candlelight?" laughed Papa.

"Yes, it is! But why did you bring that jar to the table?" asked Laura.

"Well, I want to show you a few things about a candle and its flame. Blow gently on the candle. Try not to blow it out like you do with the candles on your birthday cake."

Laura blew like Papa had asked.

"What did you see about the flame when you did that?"

"It wiggled," said Laura.

"Right. Did it go out?" asked Papa.

"No," said Laura. "The flame did wave back and forth a bit, but it didn't go out."

"Why?"

"I didn't blow hard enough," she finished.

Papa cut a square piece of cardboard so it could fit into the jar. He lit another candle. After it burned awhile, he dripped hot wax onto the cardboard. He blew out the candle and placed the bottom of the candle into the hot wax. Papa held onto the candle to keep it steady and waited until the wax cooled. After this, he put the cardboard and candle into the jar and lit the candle.

Papa asked Laura to blow at the sides of the jar. "Blow as hard as you can to put the candle out. Tell me what happened and why?" he asked.

Laura blew and blew at the sides of the jar, trying to blow out the candle. "The candle didn't go out and the flame didn't wiggle like it did before. I think the sides of the jar kept the flame from going out."

"Absolutely right, Laura! Sometimes you see candles with glass all around them. This is done to prevent a strong wind from blowing them out."

Papa handed the saucer to Laura. "I want you to put this saucer on top of the jar. Watch what happens," he said.

As Laura watched, the flame got smaller and then went out. "The candle went out. What happened?" she asked.

"When something burns, Laura, it needs air so that it can keep on burning. Where did the burning candle get the air?"

"There was air in the jar when I put the saucer on top."

"Right. Then why did the candle go out?"

Laura thought for a minute. "Was the air in the jar used up?" she asked.

"Yes, that's it. The candle used the air trapped in the jar to keep on burning. When that air was used up, the flame went out. No more air could get into the jar because of the saucer," Papa explained.

Papa took the saucer off the top of the jar. He brought some baking soda, vinegar, an eyedropper, and a cup to the table.

"Laura, use a teaspoon to sprinkle about four or five spoonfuls of baking soda around the bottom of the jar," he said.

After she did this, Papa lit the candle in the jar. "Now Laura, pour some vinegar into this cup. Only put in about ¼ cup of vinegar. Use the eyedropper to draw up some vinegar," he said.

She drew the vinegar up into the eyedropper. "What now?" she asked.

"Squeeze the vinegar along the inside of the jar. Let it run down the side to the bottom. You may have to add a second eyedropper full of vinegar. Wait a bit. Tell me what you see."

"After I put the vinegar into the jar, it started to bubble up. Later the candle went out. What happened?" she asked.

"The vinegar and baking soda changed each other. They made a gas that is not air. This gas pushed the air out of the jar. You remember, I said before that when something burns it needs air."

"Actually, air is made up of several gases. One of the gases in air is **oxygen**. This gas is the one that helps anything burning to keep on burning. Since the **oxygen** was gone from the jar, the candle went out," he explained.

"Wow! That was cool!" smiled Laura.

"One final thing, Laura. Have you ever seen a fire extinguisher?"

"Yes. Daddy has one in the garage," she said.

"Do you know what a fire extinguisher does?"

"Laura said, "I've seen them used on TV. They put out fires."

"Excellent, Laura! What we just did with the baking soda and vinegar is very similar to what happens when a fire extinguisher puts out a fire. If you use the extinguisher the right way, the chemicals inside it mix together. They make the same gas that you made with the baking soda and vinegar. When the fire extinguisher sprays this gas onto a fire, the gas pushes the **oxygen** away from the flames. Since there is no **oxygen** near the flames, the fire goes out."

"Thanks, Papa. I liked that!" she said.

After Laura ate her cookies, she went to the family room to play.

Papa cleaned up the table and put things away. Then he went to the family room to take a nap.

The Rainbow

It was a lovely spring afternoon. Laura and Grandpa were sitting on the front porch. A light rain shower had fallen earlier.

Papa looked up from reading his book and said, "Look, Laura, do you see what I see?"

"I see a rainbow!" said Laura.

"Isn't it pretty? Would you like to learn some things about a rainbow?" Papa asked.

"Yes, Papa." Laura agreed.

"OK, first let's talk about light from the sun. This light is called 'white light' because it has all the different colors in it. When this light comes to the earth from the sun, all the different colors are moving at the same speed," said Papa.

"When white light moves through glass or water, the different colors in white light travel at slightly different speeds. The speeds of all the colors slow down a little. Violet light slows down the most. Red light slows down the least. The speeds of all the other colors slow down in between the speeds of violet and red. The colors separate from each other because of these changes in their speeds," he explained.

"Here is a picture of white light entering a piece of glass from the left. Because the different colors slow down, the picture shows the colors separating from each other. The red light, since it travels the fastest, is not bent much. Because the violet light travels the slowest, it is bent more. Can you name all the colors starting at the top, Laura?" Papa asked.

"Red, Orange, Yellow, Green, Blue, and Violet," Laura said.

"Very good, Laura! Now look at the rainbow again. The colors you see there are not as bright as those in the picture with the piece of glass. Starting with the color on the left, can you tell me what colors you see as you look to the right?"

"Violet, blue, green, yellow, orange, and red," answered Laura.

"Excellent! Now you and I know there are no pieces of glass floating in the sky to slow down the white light. What do you think is in the sky that is slowing down the different colors?" Papa asked.

"Could it be drops of water from the rain?" asked Laura.

"That's it!" smiled Papa. "The raindrops or tiny bits of moisture left over from the rain are floating in the sky. They are producing the rainbow you see. Sometimes you can also see a rainbow in the mist around a waterfall," said Papa.

"Tell me, Laura, what two things are needed for you to see a rainbow?" Papa asked.

"Do you mean sunshine and raindrops?" answered Laura.

"Yes, would you like to learn a little more about rainbows?" Papa asked.

"Sure, but I hope it isn't too hard!" laughed Laura.

"I'll try to keep it simple," said Papa. "You mentioned the need for sunlight. I want to tell you that you will not see a rainbow between 10:00 in the morning to about 3:00 in the afternoon. The sun is too high in the sky. To see a rainbow, the sunlight must come into the moisture drops at a low angle. This will happen a few hours after sunrise or a few hours before sunset. Also, the sun will be at your back when you look at the rainbow," he explained.

"Something else I want to show you. Here is a picture of a rainbow. Look carefully and tell me if you notice anything else," he asked.

"Is that another rainbow I see, Papa?" Laura asked.

"Absolutely! The first rainbow on the left is called the first or **primary** rainbow. The one on the right is called the second or **secondary** rainbow," he explained.

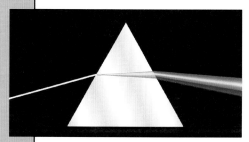

"OK, I've got it," said Laura.

"Good. Do you see that the second rainbow is not as bright as the first one?" Papa pointed out.

"Yes I do," answered Laura.

"Now look only at the first rainbow. Starting on the left, tell me the colors you see as you move to the right," said Papa.

Laura named the colors, "Violet, blue, green, yellow, orange, and red."

"Very good," said Papa. "Now I want you to list the colors of the second rainbow, but it may be hard because it is so faint. Starting on the left, tell me the colors you see as you move to the right on this second rainbow."

Laura named these colors, "Red, orange, yellow, green, and blue but I don't see the violet."
"Very good. It's OK you didn't see the violet because it's very faint. Is there anything different about how these colors are arranged?" he asked.

"They are backwards from each other, Papa," Laura answered.

"That's a good way to put it, Laura," he agreed, "I would say the colors are reversed."

"Why is that?" Laura wondered.

"That's a hard question to answer now. It has to do with reflections of the sunlight and colors inside the raindrops. When you are older and study science, you will learn more about this. Is that OK, Laura?" Papa asked.

"That's OK with me, Papa," Laura smiled.

"To finish up our story about rainbows, I want to ask you to look for something. You might not be able to see this for many years. Are you ready for this challenge?" Papa now smiled.

"I like challenges—they're fun. What is it?" she asked.

"Many years ago, when I was in college, I read a book about rainbows. It said that if the conditions were just right, I might be able to see a third or **tertiary** rainbow."

"Since then, whenever I see a rainbow, I've always looked for the second and third rainbows and many times I have seen a secondary rainbow," Papa said.

"I did see a third rainbow once, but didn't know it at the time. This happened because the book I read in college didn't tell me where to look for the third rainbow. Many years later, I found out that the **tertiary** rainbow is not in the same direction as the first and second ones. You have to turn around and look towards the sun. So whenever you see a rainbow, look for the **secondary** rainbow and then turn around and look towards the sun. The third rainbow will be very, very faint. It will be harder to see than the second rainbow, but maybe the conditions will be just right for you to see it. I hope that someday you see this, because it is very pretty!" Papa said.

After this, Laura gave her Papa a big hug and kiss and then went to her room and drew a beautiful rainbow to give to her Nana.

The Window

 One day Laura came home from school with her friend, Luca. Grandpa was in the kitchen having a cup of tea, reading his book.

"Hi, Laura, how are you?" Papa asked.

"I'm fine, Papa. This is my friend, Luca. He lives around the corner on the next street. We're in the same class at school."

"I'm pleased to meet you, Luca. I hear you are one of Laura's good friends."

"Nice to meet you, sir!" said Luca. "Laura's told me about some of your stories."

Papa said, "Just before you two came in, I was drinking my tea and looking out the window. Come over here and tell me what you see when you look through the window."

Luca looked out and said, "I see a tree, the grass, and some flowers."

Laura added, "There's Sherlock, our dog, running around. I also see Daddy's shed where he keeps a lot of his tools."

"Very good, you two. You saw those objects because light came from them to your eyes. But before they got to your eyes, the light traveled through something. Can you tell me what that was?" asked Papa.

"When we talked about rainbows last week, I think you told me that light traveled through air," said Laura.

"You're right, but I was thinking about something else. Do you know what that might be?" he pressed.

"How about the window?" asked Luca.

"Now you've got it! What is the window made of?" asked Papa.

"Glass," answered Laura.

"Excellent, Laura! I want to talk about the glass in the window. Light can easily pass through this type of glass. Light goes through so well that objects which are found beyond it can be seen very clearly," Papa said.

"Now, let's go to the bathroom," suggested Papa.

When they got to the bathroom, Papa stopped at the door. "Look in here. Is there a window?"

"Yes," said Luca.

"What is the window made of?" Papa asked.

"Glass," said Laura and Luca together.

"Good. Is light coming through this window and is anything different about this window from the kitchen window?" he asked them.

"Light is coming into the bathroom. I can see the bathtub, sink, towels, soap, and other things, but you didn't turn on the light," said Laura.

"OK. But what about the difference?" Papa asked.

"I can't see anything on the outside like the trees or the grass," said Luca

"Very good. This glass here does let light pass through it. But it doesn't allow a clear image of any object on the outside to pass through it."

"The glass in this window is made of **glass blocks** and the glass in the kitchen was different. It had several sections called **panes,**" Papa explained.

"Let's go back to the kitchen," he said.

When they got to the kitchen, Papa opened the door.

"Look through the door. What do you see?"

Laura said, "I see Sherlock and the tool shed. I also see Isabelle's house which is behind ours."

"I see the trees, grass, and flowers again," said Luca.

"The light from these objects is traveling through something to get to your eyes. What is that?" Papa asked.

"Air, but not glass," answered Laura.

"Excellent. Now I will close the door. Can you still see those objects and if not, why not?" Papa asked.

"I don't see anything on the outside," said Laura.

"The light doesn't go through the door," added Luca.

"Very good! There are many things light cannot pass through. The door is made up of such materials and the walls of your house are also made of materials, which prevent light from passing through them," explained Papa.

"Let's go over a few things before we go any further. Before today, tell me something you knew about light and then tell me what you learned that was new," he asked.

"Well, I knew light traveled through air very easily, I learned that when we talked about the rainbow last week," said Laura. "Today I learned that light goes through other things easily, like the panes in the kitchen window."

"Good. Anything else?" asked Papa.

"Today I learned that light goes through some glass, but not so easily. In this type of glass, like glass blocks, clear images on the outside are blocked out," said Luca.

"Great. Can you tell me one more thing you learned about light?" pressed Papa.

"I learned that there are things light will not pass through at all," replied Laura.

"Excellent! I would like both of you to sit down at the table," suggested Papa.

Laura and Luca sat down, while Papa went to the fridge for some milk and apple juice. He gave Laura and Luca some milk. He poured a glass of juice for himself.

While they sat drinking, Papa said, "I am thinking of some other things I would like to show you about light. Would you like to do that?" he asked, smiling.

"Yes," said Laura and Luca.

Papa went to his bag and pulled out three plastic sheets. "Tell me, what is the color of each sheet?"

"Red, blue and green. Blue is my favorite color," said Laura.

"Red is my favorite color," said Luca.

"Very good. If you are finished with your milk, let's go into the living room. The sun will set in about an hour or so and I think there is enough light for me to show you something."

 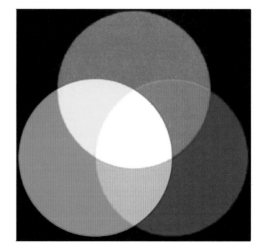

In the living room, Papa had Laura and Luca sit on chairs facing the window. "Last week I talked to you about the rainbow. Do you remember the name for the light coming to the earth from the sun and do you remember the colors it contained?" Papa asked Laura.

Laura thought for a few moments. Then she said, "I think it is called 'white light.' The sunlight has all the colors of the rainbow in it. I remember some of them. They were red, green, blue, orange, and yellow."

"Very good, but you forgot one color—violet," said Papa.

He went to the window and with scotch tape, he taped the blue sheet on the window. "Look at the sheet I just put on the window. What color do you see?" he asked them.

"Are you trying to be silly, Papa? I see blue," laughed Laura.

"Good." Then he taped the red sheet on the window near the blue one. "Look at this second sheet. Luca, tell me what color you see?"

"Red, of course," he answered.

"Perfect." Next Papa taped the green sheet on the window near the others. "Look at this sheet I just put on the window. What color do you see now?"

They both said, "Green!"

"Let me explain what is happening," offered Papa. "The sunlight has ALL the colors of the rainbow in it. The blue sheet blocks out ALL the colors except blue, so only blue light passes through it. That's why it looks blue to you," he said.

"Do you think you could explain to me about why you see red through the red sheet, Luca?" he then asked.

"I'll try. The sunlight on the outside of the window has all the colors in it. The red sheet blocks out all the colors except red. So sitting in here and looking at this sheet, I only see the red color coming through it," he answered.

"Excellent, Luca, and what do you have to say about the green one, Laura?" Papa asked. "Well it would be the same thing, only the green color would come through. Papa, I have a question. Is this why I see those pretty colors in the colored windows at the museum?"

"Absolutely, and it's great that you can think of other things you can explain by what you just learned. Those windows you saw in the museum are **stained glass** windows," he said.

"When you saw the stained glass windows, did you notice that though they let the different colors come through, you couldn't see anything on the outside of the windows?" asked Papa.

"That's right," said Laura, "I couldn't see the cars driving by on the street, even though I could hear the noise of them passing by."

"Papa, why could I hear the cars but couldn't see them?" she wondered.

"That's a good question. Would either of you like to try to answer that one? " Papa asked.

Both children sat silent for some time thinking about what they might say. Then Luca tried, "Could it be that the colored glass is made of material much like the **glass block** window in the bathroom?"

"That was just great, Luca; I couldn't have said it any better! Though the light didn't come through clearly, sound managed to get through the window and that's why you could hear the noise of the cars." Papa explained.

"I'm not sure I understand the difference between light and sound, Papa," said Laura.

"Very good point, Laura. That's a story for another time. OK?"

"Sure," she said.

As Papa took the colored sheets off the window, he said, "I have extra sheets. So here's a blue, green, and red one for you, Laura, and, Luca, I am going to give you a red, green and blue set. You can play with them. During the daytime you can hold them up to the window and see the different colors coming through them," he smiled.

"You can put a part of one over the other and see what colors come through. You could also place two over each other and see what the light looks like through two or three of the sheets," he challenged them.

"Hold them up in front of a light bulb that is turned on. See what colors come through. However, if you do this, you must be careful not to put the sheets too close to the bulb because they might melt," he cautioned.

"OK, Papa, but why would they melt?" Laura asked.

"Wow! Another good question Laura! You know how a light bulb gets very hot when it is on? The heat from the light bulb would melt the plastic sheet and then you would have to throw it out. I think it's almost time for dinner. I'm getting hungry."

"Me too," said Luca. "I have to get home for supper. Thank you for the story" he waved goodbye to them.

"You're welcome, Luca. I hope I see you again and soon," said Papa.

"I'm hungry too," said Laura, "let's go eat."

Roses are Red, Violets are Blue

O n a beautiful spring day, Papa walked into Laura's front yard where she and Austin were playing "fetch the ball" with Sherlock, her dog.

"Hi, Laura! Hi, Austin!" he said. "Isn't it a nice day? The weather is just great."

"Hi, Papa," she smiled, "I just love this spring weather."

"We're having fun playing with Sherlock," said Austin.

"I see that," said Papa. "Look at all those lovely flowers blooming in the garden. I think spring with all the pretty flowers is the best time of the year."

"Laura, let me have the ball for a minute. I want to show you something."

Standing about five feet from the front steps, Papa lobbed the ball gently towards the steps. It bounced straight back and he caught it.

He then took the ball and tossed it at the steps, but at an angle. It bounced off into the yard and Sherlock raced off to get it.

"I'm sure both of you have done something like this, bounced a ball off the side of the

34

garage or the back wall of your house, haven't you?" Papa asked.

"Oh, yes! Many times," Laura nodded.

"I do that all the time when I play basketball," said Austin. "I bounce the ball off the backboard."

"I would like to describe what I just did with a word you may not have heard before. All right?"

"Sure, go ahead," Laura said.

"What I did with the ball was to **reflect** it off of the stairs and the first time, it **reflected** straight back to me. The second time, when it hit the stairs at an angle, it **reflected** off into the yard."

"If you don't mind, I would like to show you something else. Austin, go sit on the porch. Laura and I are going into the house to bring some things out," said Papa going up the stairs.

"Fine, Papa! I'll let Sherlock play with the ball while I sit on the porch," said Austin.

A few minutes later Papa and Laura came back. They were carrying a stack of towels, which they placed on a small table.

As he sat down Papa said, "Tell me Laura, why do you use a towel?"

"Are you being silly again, Papa? I use a towel to dry my hands and face when I wash them. I also use a towel to dry myself when I take a bath."

"Good," said Papa. "Austin, have you ever used a sheet of plastic or your raincoat to dry your hands and face?"

"No," answered Austin.

"Why not?" asked Papa.

"Boy, you are really being silly today Papa," Austin laughed. "Because a plastic sheet or my raincoat wouldn't soak up the water," he explained.

"Very good! The material of these towels soaks up water very well. I would say that the towel **absorbs** the water, while the plastic and raincoat do not **absorb** water."

"I think I understand that," said Laura.

Then Papa said, "I'm now going to shift our thinking a bit. A few weeks ago I told you a story about 'The Rainbow,' do you remember what we called the light coming from the sun to the earth?"

"Yes, it's called 'white light,'" Austin said. "It has the colors of the rainbow in it."

"I believe these colors are red, orange, yellow, green, blue, and violet. Did I get it right, Papa?" asked Laura.

"Perfect! Here is something I didn't mention before. The sun is a source of light. We call it an **emitter**. Light bulbs or lasers are also **emitters** because they produce light."

"The earth, moon, and most things you see are not emitters of light. They are **reflectors** of light. They do not produce light, they **reflect** light that comes from an **emitter**. Does that make sense?" Papa asked.

"Yes, Papa, but what about the sky at night? When I see all those pretty stars in the sky, am I looking at **emitters** or **reflectors**?" Austin asked.

"Wow, that's a GREAT question! You have just opened the door to talking about all the many objects out there in our universe. This gets us into the study of astronomy. When you get to high school or college, you will learn much more about astronomy," he replied.

"However, to answer your question, Austin, let me say this:"

1. Most of the objects you see in the night sky are **emitters** of light. We call these objects stars because they produce light.

2. There are other objects seen in the night sky that are **reflectors** of light. Some of these **reflecting** objects are called planets, others are called moons. They do not produce light themselves but reflect it when it comes from an **emitter**.

"Is this OK?" he asked.

"I think so, but maybe I'll have another question later," Austin said.

"That's OK! Let me get back to talking about these towels. Look at this green towel. It is, as you now know, a reflector of light. It also **absorbs** or soaks up some of the colors in white light. It **absorbs** the red, orange, yellow, blue and violet colors. It only **reflects** the green color. That is why the towel looks green to us. OK, Laura?" he asked.

"Gosh, that's a lot, Papa! But I think I understand," said Laura.

"OK, Austin, let's see if you got it. Tell me, why does that beautiful rose out in your garden look red?" Papa asked.

"I'll try. The rose is not an **emitter** of light, but it is a **reflector** of light. The 'white light' from the sun shines on the rose, but the rose does not reflect all of the colors. It absorbs most of the colors in 'white light' and only **reflects** the red color," Austin explained.

"Excellent, Austin! Most of the things we see here on earth, we see because of **reflection**. The color of the violets you see in the garden is because of reflection. The color of Sherlock is because of reflection. The color of this green towel is because of reflection. And so on," said Papa.

"Just a few more things I would like to show you about colors, OK?"

"Sure Papa, go ahead," said Laura and Austin together.

Papa pulled three pictures out of his pocket. He handed one to Laura. "The first picture is of 'white light' shining on a red ball. Notice that the ball has absorbed all the colors except red. We see the ball as a red ball because of reflection."

The second picture he gave to Austin. "This is a picture of the same red ball. But only red light is shining on it. The ball reflects the red color of the incoming light. It does not absorb any other colors because there were no other colors present in the incoming light," Papa explained.

Papa held up the third picture, so both Laura and Austin could see it. "This picture is of the same ball in which only green light is shining on it. There is no red color in the incoming light. The ball cannot **reflect** a red color, since it is not present. The ball **reflects** no color. The ball looks dark against the green background."

"Here's a challenge for you two. I took this picture of the new puppy down at the firehouse. Tell me why I see white fur, black spots, and a red helmet."

Laura looked at the picture and said, "He's cute! Here goes. 'White light' is shining on this puppy so you could take its picture. Some of his fur **reflects** all the colors, so we see this fur as white. In other places, the fur

absorbs all the colors and doesn't **reflect** any colors. These places we see as spots on the puppy."

Austin said, "His helmet looks red because it **reflected** only the red color of the incoming light. It **absorbed** all the other colors."

"Excellent," said Papa, "just one more thing about colors I want to tell both of you."

"Everything I have told you today and in the earlier stories about 'The Rainbow' and 'The Window' has been about light coming to us from the sun which is an **emitter**. This light, as you know, is 'white light,' which contains red, orange, yellow, green, blue, and violet colors."

"Now, if you went to your art classes and began mixing all the colored paints together, you wouldn't get this 'white color.' Instead, you would get a muddy, dark-brown paint."

"Mixing the **pigments** in paints, or dyes, is different than mixing colors of light. **Pigments** are tiny particles that **absorb** certain colors," Papa explained.

"Wow, that's a lot to remember," said Laura. "I think I'm ready to go back and play 'fetch' with Sherlock."

"Me too," said Austin.

"You're right," said Papa, "that's enough for today! Have fun with Sherlock. I'm going to put these towels back in the closet. See both of you later when we have dinner."

Epsom Towers

It was a sunny but cool Sunday afternoon. Laura was working on her homework when Papa and Austin walked into her room. Papa was carrying a small bag.

"Hi, Papa, how are you today?" asked Laura. "Hi, Austin."

"I'm just fine. How about you, Laura?" Papa smiled. Austin said hello to Laura.

"I'm good. What have you got in the bag, Papa?" she asked.

Papa said, "I've got some special salt and I want to show you something. We'll have to do this in the kitchen. Are you finished with your homework?"

"Just about. I need only five more minutes," answered Laura.

"OK! Come to the kitchen when you're finished. We'll be setting everything up," said Papa.

When Laura came into the kitchen, she found some paper towels, a box of Epsom Salt, two small clear glasses, a cup, a measuring cup, string, aluminum foil, and paper clips on the table.

"Laura, would you please measure out 3/4 cup of Epsom Salt?" asked Papa. "I'm going to get a cup of boiling water from the kettle on the stove. Now Laura and Austin, don't ever try this by yourself. Get your Mommy or Daddy to help you do what I am doing now—do you understand?"

"Yes Papa, I know what you mean," said Laura and Austin nodded.

He came to the table with the cup of very hot water and poured in the Epsom Salt from the measuring cup. "Austin, carefully stir the water and salt with a spoon and tell me when all the salt has dissolved," instructed Papa.

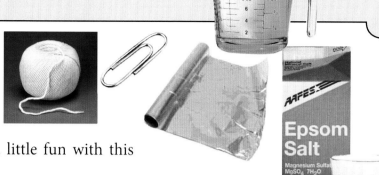

After Austin did this, Papa divided the solution from the cup into each of the two glasses.

"Laura, would you like to have a little fun with this experiment?" Papa asked.

"I think I would like that," smiled Laura.

"Good," Papa smiled. "Laura, put two drops of red food coloring in one glass. Austin, put two drops of green food coloring in the other glass and carefully stir each with a clean spoon."

After they did this, Papa took a 12-14 inch piece of string and tied a large paper clip at each end. Rolling up the string he dropped it and the clips into one of the glasses.

"Let's allow the string to soak in the solution for about five to ten minutes and while this is happening, let's get the other part of the experiment ready. Laura, tear off about a twelve-inch piece of aluminum foil. Flatten it out and place it on this corner of the counter," Papa instructed.

"Austin, please bring those two glasses over to the counter and set them on the foil about four to six inches apart."

Papa took the string out of the glass where it was soaking. He dropped one paper clip back into the glass and placed the second clip into the other glass.

"The paper clips will hold the string down in each glass," Papa explained. "The rest of the string should be drooping between the glasses. However, we don't want the hanging string to touch the foil. Move the distance between the glasses so that the bottom of the string is about two inches above the aluminum foil."

Laura adjusted the glasses as Papa had directed. After this, he said, "We need to let this 'work' for awhile, so let's all go for a walk to the park."

"Sure, Papa," said Laura. "Wait a minute while I go upstairs to get my sweater." Laura and

Austin went for a walk to the park with Papa.

An hour later, the three returned and went into the kitchen to see how their hanging string was doing. "Look at the foil below the lowest part of the string. Do you see anything?" Papa asked.

"I see some drops of water dripping down from the string onto the foil," said Austin.

"Is that all, Papa?" asked Laura.

"No, this is just the beginning of what we want to see. We'll have to wait until tomorrow or the day after, before it is finished," he said.

Two days later when Laura came home from school, Papa was at the kitchen table having a cup of coffee. Austin was also there drinking a glass of milk. "Hi, Laura. Why don't you go over to the counter and look at our hanging string? What do you see?"

"Wow, what is this?" she said, surprised. "On the foil, I see some stuff that rises up like a little tower and I also see some stuff hanging from the string. What happened?"

"OK, let me try to explain what we have done."

1. *Remember we dissolved the Epsom Salt into very hot, boiling water. This dissolved a lot of the salt into the water. More salt than if we had dissolved it in cold water. We call this a* **saturated** *solution. This means that there is extra salt dissolved into the water.*

2. *After this, we soaked the string into this* **saturated** *solution.*

3. We hung the string from the glasses with the ends of the string still in the solution. This kept the string moist so it could continue to soak up more of the solution.

4. Drops of this solution fell from the lowest point of the sagging string between the glasses onto the foil.

5. *The water in the drops that fell on the foil evaporated. But the Epsom Salt that was dissolved in the solution did not evaporate. It remained behind as a solid* **crystal**. *The deposited* **crystals** *you see formed this tower on the foil.*

6. *A similar thing happened at the low point on the string. Some of the water there evaporated and left behind a deposit of Epsom Salt* **crystals** *that you see on the string."*

"That was neat!" said Laura.

"I want to mention one final thing, but it will involve two new, very big words. Is that OK with both of you?" asked Papa.

"That's all right. We like to learn new words," said Austin and Laura agreed.

"Someday your Mother and Father might take you to visit a cave. Caves are found all over the world and in our country there are caves in 37 of the 50 states," Papa said.

"In some of these caves, you will see giant rock formations hanging from the ceiling. They look like icicles that you see in winter. These hanging rock formations are called **stalactites**. You will also see, growing up from the floor of the cave, rock forms called **stalagmites**."

"Both of these rock formations were made by a natural process that is similar to what we did with our Epsom Salt solution."

"That's great, Papa," said Laura.

"Thank you for showing us this!" said Austin.

"You're welcome! Now Laura, you and Austin please clean up these glasses and everything else. Throw the string and foil away."

"If you want to keep the paper clips, rinse them off and let them dry before putting them away. I think I'll watch some TV before dinner."

CPSIA information can be obtained
at www.ICGtesting.com
Printed in the USA
BVXC01n1219220315
391976BV00003B/4